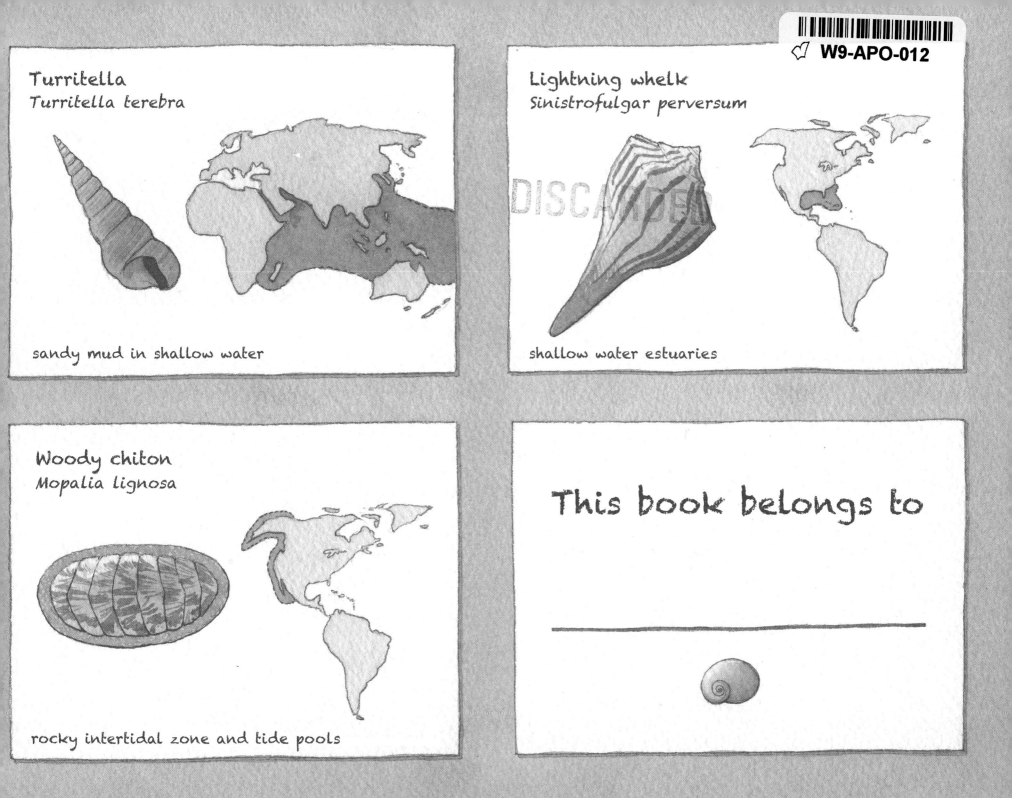

Turritella
Turritella terebra

sandy mud in shallow water

Lightning whelk
Sinistrofulgar perversum

shallow water estuaries

Woody chiton
Mopalia lignosa

rocky intertidal zone and tide pools

This book belongs to

Seashells
More Than a Home

Melissa Stewart • Illustrated by Sarah S. Brannen

Charlesbridge

Every day, seashells wash up on beaches all over Earth, like treasures from a secret world beneath the waves. Spiraled or spiky, round or ridged, shells come in all sorts of shapes and sizes, and all the colors of the rainbow. That's because seashells have so many different jobs to do.

Seashells can rise and sink like a submarine . . .

A nautilus floats because most of its shell is filled with a lightweight gas. To dive down it pumps water into its shell. When the nautilus wants to rise toward the surface, it lets water flow out of its shell.

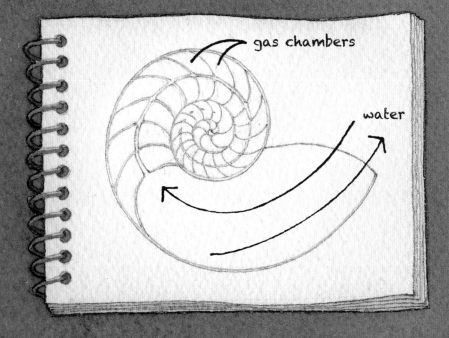

gas chambers

water

or hold steady like an anchor.

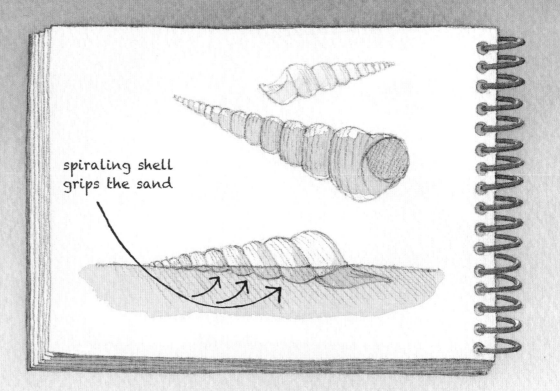

spiraling shell
grips the sand

A turritella nestles into the soft, sandy seafloor and filters tiny bits of food out of the water washing over its body. This sea snail can stay in one spot for weeks at a time because its screw-shaped shell grips its surroundings. The shell holds the little mollusk in place.

Seashells can pry like a crowbar . . .

When a hungry lightning whelk spots a clam, it climbs on top of its prey. The hunter slips the edge of its shell between the two halves, or valves, of the clam's shell. Slowly, slowly, the whelk pries the clam's shell open. Then it slurps up the soft, slimy animal inside.

or bore holes like a drill bit.

sharp ridges

To stay safe from predators, an angelwing clam tunnels into the seabed. As the mollusk spins in circles, the rough ridges on its shell scrape and grind the sand, mud, and clay around it. Over time the clam wears away a burrow up to three feet deep.

Seashells can flit and flutter like a butterfly . . .

direction
of travel

water jets

A scallop spends most of its time lying on the ocean floor. But when a predator attacks, the scallop claps its valves together to propel itself out of harm's way. Some kinds of scallops hop and zigzag across the ocean floor. Others dodge and dart, or skim and glide through the water.

or curl up tight like an armadillo.

Like a knight's suit of armor, a chiton's shell has flexible plates that make it easier for the mollusk to move. When a hungry sea otter plucks a chiton off a rock, the plates come in handy. They let the mollusk roll itself into a ball to protect its soft body.

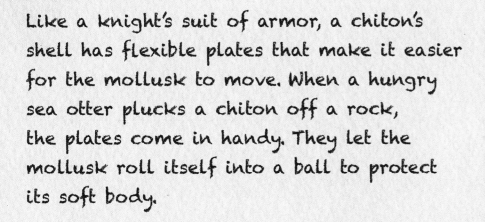

chiton

armadillo

Seashells can let in light like a window . . .

Some areas of a heart cockle shell let sunlight pass through. That's good news for the tiny algae that live inside the clam's shell. Like plants, algae need sunlight to make food. It's also good news for the heart cockle because it eats some of its tiny tenants.

or belch out waste like a ship's smokestack.

All animals make waste material, and they need to get rid of it. An abalone's wastes escape through a row of holes that runs along one side of its shell.

holes where wastes exit

shiny inside of abalone shell

Seashells can wear disguises like a spy . . .

thorny oyster shell without hitchhikers

The spines on a thorny oyster's shell are the perfect home for sponges, algae, and other small creatures. As these hitchhikers grow on the outer surface of the oyster, they hide its shell from hungry hunters.

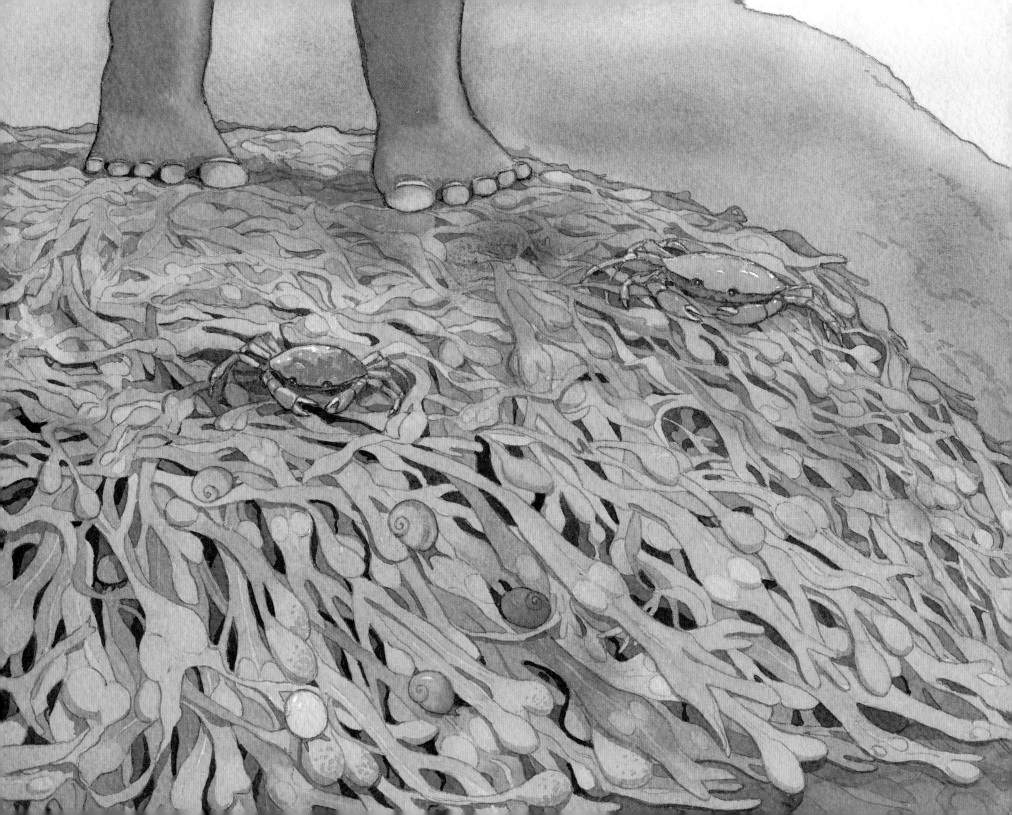

or hide in plain sight like a soldier in camo clothing.

A flat periwinkle's shell matches the color
of the seaweed it lives on. This makes it
hard for enemies to spot the little sea snail.

Seashells can open up like your mouth . . .

When mussels feel safe they open
their shells and suck up tiny bits
of food floating in the water.

and close quickly like your eyelids.

But when mussels sense danger, they snap their shells shut to protect their soft insides.

Seashells can send out a warning
like the signal from a lighthouse . . .

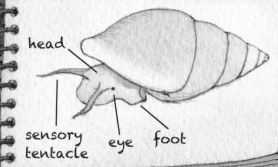

head

sensory
tentacle   eye   foot

When a yellow-coated clusterwink senses danger, it produces a flickering light. The mollusk's shell magnifies and spreads the light, creating a green glow that tells enemies to keep their distance.

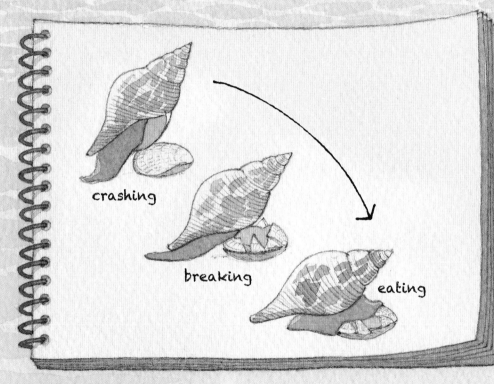

crashing

breaking

eating

A tulip snail's favorite food is other mollusks.
When it spots a tasty clam, it hurls itself at
the prey. Crash! Boom! Bang! The tulip snail
keeps slamming against the clam until the
clam's shell shatters. Then the hunter slurps
down its meal.

or smash other shells like crashing waves against the shore.

But most of all, hard, strong seashells make good homes. They protect like a fortress, keeping mollusks safe in their underwater world.

Kinds of Seashells

Many ocean animals have shells, but the word *seashell* usually refers to the hard covering that protects a mollusk. A mollusk is a soft-bodied, legless animal. Many mollusks move around on a muscular foot. The five largest groups of mollusks are:

Bivalves

Clams, mussels, oysters, and scallops are all bivalves. Their shells have two halves, or valves, that can open and close. Some bivalves burrow in the sand. Others attach themselves to hard surfaces. Most bivalves filter tiny bits of food from the water.

Cephalopods

Squids, octopuses, and cuttlefish are all cephalopods. But the nautilus is the only cephalopod with a shell on the outside of its body. All cephalopods swim through the sea in search of prey.

Chitons

A chiton's shell has eight overlapping plates. Chitons live in shallow ocean water. They crawl along the rocky bottom, grazing on algae and sponges.

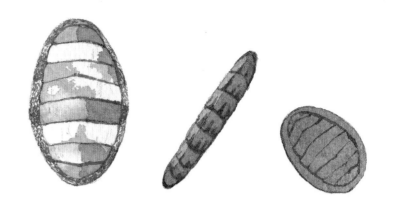

Gastropods

Gastropods, or snails, are the largest group of mollusks. Most snails have a coiled shell. They can live in the ocean, in fresh water, or on land. They eat a wide variety of foods.

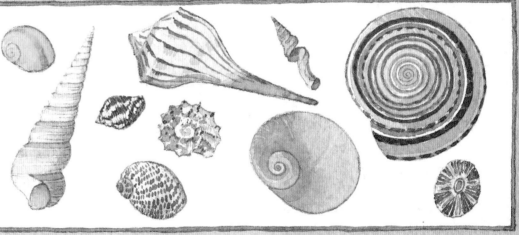

Scaphopods

A scaphopod, or tusk shell, has a long, tube-shaped shell that is open at both ends. These animals burrow into soft areas of the ocean floor and catch tiny creatures with their threadlike tentacles.

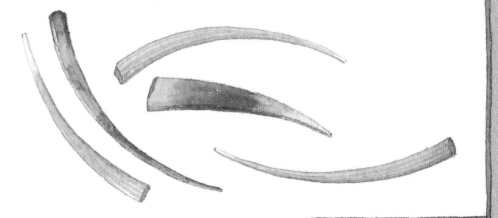

Author's Note

The idea for this book popped into my mind when I saw Sarah S. Brannen's gorgeous sketches for our book *Feathers: Not Just for Flying*. On the final page a boy is running along the beach as gulls soar overhead. I imagined that boy shifting his attention from the birds above him to the seashells scattered along the sandy shore, and then heading off on a new voyage of discovery. I connected with that boy because, in many ways, he was me.

I've been fascinated by shells since childhood, when I spent summer vacations beachcombing on Cape Cod, Massachusetts. As an adult I've explored beaches all over the world, from Costa Rica and the Galápagos Islands to Hawaii, Great Britain, and Kenya. I began my research for this book by looking through all my travel journals. Then I read every shell book and article I could find. I scoured the internet and spoke to a half-dozen scientists. After two years of work, I came to a sad conclusion. I couldn't find enough information to write the book. I'd have to give up.

But then, a year later, I went to a seashell exhibit at the Harvard Museum of Natural History in Cambridge, Massachusetts, and found a newly published seashell book in the bookstore. I couldn't believe it! Not only did the book have examples I could use, it helped me develop a whole new way of searching for information. After just a few more weeks of research, I was finally ready to write.

—Melissa Stewart

Illustrator's Note

Like Melissa I have loved seashells since I was little. One of my earliest memories is of finding coquina shells on the beach in Florida. I called them "butterfly shells," but I know now that they are species of clam. I loved the way the rich, varied colors echoed the colors of the sunset over the ocean.

Illustrating Melissa's book *Feathers: Not Just for Flying* was a dream come true. I had seen the manuscript in its early stages and I was thrilled to have the opportunity to bring the book to life. Even before it was published, I hoped that Melissa would write another, similar book about seashells. I feel very lucky that I got to illustrate this book, too!

In researching all the shells mentioned in this book, I was able to take a trip to the beach in Captiva, Florida. I've seen some of the mollusks, like mussels and scallops, all my life during visits to the shores of Maine. And I also immersed myself in video documentaries about life under the ocean, trying to visualize what all the animals in this book look like when they're at home in the water.

I've been drawing seashells since I was little. They are surprisingly tricky to draw, but I hope that readers who encounter this book will bring a sketchbook to the beach and give it a try. You never see something as clearly as when you try to draw it.

—Sarah S. Brannen

Continue Your Exploration

Arthur, Alex. *Shell*. New York: Dorling Kindersley, 2013.

"How Do Seashells Form?" *Highlights for Children*. April 2013, p. 24.

Zoehfeld, Kathleen Weidner. *What Lives in a Shell?* New York: HarperCollins, 2015.

Selected Sources, Author

Dance, S. Peter. *Shells*. New York: Dorling Kindersley, 2002.

Deheyn, Dimitri D., and Nerida G. Wilson. "Bioluminescent Signals Spatially Amplified by Wavelength-Specific Diffusion Through the Shell of a Marine Snail." *Proceedings of the Royal Society*, June 10, 2011, pp. 2112–2121.

Feifarek, Brian P. "Spines and Epibionts as Antipredator Defenses in the Thorny Oyster *Spondylus americanus* Hermann." *Journal of Experimental Marine Biology and Ecology*, February 17, 1987, pp. 39–56.

Gabbi, Giorgio. *Shells: Guide to the Jewels of the Sea*. New York: Abbeville Press Publishers, 2000.

Harasewych, M. G., and Fabio Moretzsohn. *The Book of Shells: A Life-Size Guide to Identifying and Classifying Six Hundred Seashells*. Chicago: University of Chicago Press, 2010.

Hill, Leonard. *Shells: Treasures of the Sea*. New York: Hugh Lauter Levin Associates, 1996.

Mollusks: Shelled Masters of the Marine Realm. Exhibition. Harvard Museum of Natural History, Cambridge, MA, Summer 2015.

Scales, Helen. *Spirals in Time: The Secret Life and Curious Afterlife of Seashells*. New York: Bloomsbury, 2015.

Starosta, Paul, and Jacques Senders. *Shells*. Buffalo, NY: Firefly Books, 2007.

Vermeij, Geerat J. *A Natural History of Shells*. Princeton, NJ: Princeton University Press, 1993.

Personal observations along the beaches of Aruba; Costa Rica; Florida; the Galápagos Islands, Ecuador; Great Britain; Hawaii; Kenya; Maine; Massachusetts; Vancouver Island, Canada; and the Yucatán Peninsula, Mexico.

Selected Sources, Illustrator

Bailey-Matthews National Shell Museum, Sanibel, Florida.

The Blue Planet: Seas of Life. Dolby digital 2.0 stereo, 394 minutes, Burbank, CA: BBC Video, 2002, DVD.

Harasewych, M. G., and Fabio Moretzsohn. *The Book of Shells: A Life-Size Guide to Identifying and Classifying Six Hundred Seashells*. Chicago: University of Chicago Press, 2010.

Planet Earth. Dolby digital 5.1, 550 minutes, Burbank, CA: BBC Worldwide Americas, 2011, DVD.

Scales, Helen. *Spirals in Time: The Secret Life and Curious Afterlife of Seashells*. New York: Bloomsbury, 2015.

To Sarah S. Brannen, a great artist and a great friend—M. S.

To my niece Katherine Alwan, who helped me find most of the shells in this book—S. S. B.

Published by Charlesbridge
85 Main Street
Watertown, MA 02472
(617) 926-0329
www.charlesbridge.com

Library of Congress Cataloging-in-Publication Data
Names: Stewart, Melissa, author. | Brannen, Sarah S., illustrator.
Title: Seashells: more than a home / Melissa Stewart; illustrated by Sarah S. Brannen.
Description: Watertown, MA: Charlesbridge, [2019] | Includes bibliographical references.
Identifiers: LCCN 2017056289 | ISBN 9781580898102 (reinforced for library use) | ISBN 9781632896599 (ebook pdf)
Subjects: LCSH: Mollusks—Juvenile literature. | Shells—Juvenile literature.
Classification: LCC QL405.2 .S74 2019 | DDC 594.147/7—dc23 LC record available at https://lccn.loc.gov/2017056289

Printed in China
(hc) 10 9 8 7 6 5 4 3 2 1

Illustrations done in watercolor on Arches 300 lb. bright white cold press paper
Display type set in Chicken Basket by Font Diner
Text type set in Frogster by Typotheticals
Color separations by Colourscan Print Co Pte Ltd, Singapore
Printed by 1010 Printing International Limited in Huizhou, Guangdong, China
Production supervision by Brian G. Walker
Designed by Diane M. Earley

Mollusk habitats and ranges . . .

Heart cockle
Corculum cardissa

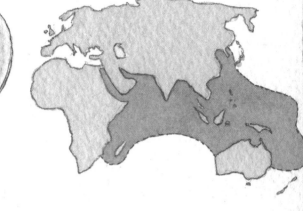

sandy bottom in shallow water

Flat periwinkle
Littorina obtusata

rocky shores, usually among seaweed

Horse mussel
Modiolus modiolus

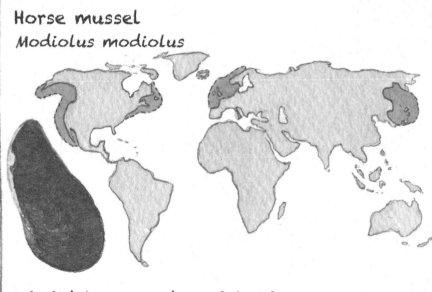

intertidal zone and coastal waters